Small PATCHWORK Projects

With Step-by-Step Instructions and Full-Size Templates

Barbara Brondolo

Dover Publications, Inc.
New York

Published in Canada by General Publishing Company, Ltd., 30 Lesmill Road, Don Mills, Toronto, Ontario.
Published in the United Kingdom by Constable and Company, Ltd., 10 Orange Street, London WC2H 7EG.

Small Patchwork Projects with Step-by-Step Instructions and Full-Size Templates is a new work, first published by Dover Publications, Inc., in 1981.

International Standard Book Number: 0-486-24030-4
Library of Congress Catalog Card Number: 80-69323

Manufactured in the United States of America
Dover Publications, Inc.
180 Varick Street
New York, N.Y. 10014

Contents

Introduction   1

Hostess Apron with Three Borders   4

Pennsylvania Dutch Eyeglass Case   6

Wall Hangings   8

Evening Bag   10

Gold Fish—Blue Fish Baby Bibs   12

Crown Jewels Tote Bag   14

Crazy Quilt Grow Chart   16

Basket of Flowers
    Placemats, Napkins and Centerpiece   18

Drunkard's Path Pillow   20

Baby Blocks Floor Pillow   22

Carpenter's Wheel Sofa Throw   24

Sunburst Kitchen Combination   26

Introduction

The idea of compiling a handbook of quilting projects for the mobile, active life of today's craft worker grew out of a course that I have been giving in an adult-education center for the past few years. The people who turned up once a week after a day of work—or managing their households—to participate in the revival of this old craft were an extraordinary group with special needs. They ranged in age from the late teens to the senior citizen; in background, from student to administrator. Among this group were nurses, teachers, secretaries, executives and full and part-time homemakers. A few lived in homes large enough to set aside one room for hobbies; most lived in smaller homes or apartments. Most wanted projects small enough to take out of a knitting bag so that they could quilt on their lunch hour or during their free time.

Unlike their colonial ancestors, who quilted from childhood and worked on large frames in family or community style, the modern quilters learned to quilt as adults and generally worked at their new skill independently or in groups of two. While earlier women quilted to make necessary and useful household items, these modern women wanted to emulate the taste and skill of the past while adding a unique and luxurious object to their wardrobes or homes.

The projects assembled here were all designed to fill the need for small, frameless, portable patchwork projects that today's life style demands. Most of them require only a few yards of fabric, some polyester fiberfill and a little practice. Many of them can be completed in a few hours. Although I have always encouraged the use of the sewing machine, I have found that many of my students elect to work by hand, finding the activity surprisingly relaxing. I have therefore given instructions for both methods wherever possible.

If you have always wanted to learn how to do patchwork but have been fearful of undertaking the making of an entire quilt, these projects will serve as a good introduction to the craft. Many of my students were able to complete quilts with confidence and success after first making a few smaller items.

Before beginning to work on the patchwork project of your choice, read through the general instructions.

Templates

All of the pattern pieces used in making these projects are given in actual-size templates printed on heavyweight paper in the template section of this book. Locate the designated template and carefully cut it out. It is important that all templates be cut out carefully because if they are not accurate, the patchwork pieces will not fit together. Use a pair of good-sized sharp scissors, a single-edged razor blade or an X-Acto knife. Be careful not to blunt the fine corners of the triangles.

Choice of Materials

The color schemes specified are only meant as guidelines. Feel free to use your own color choices. When choosing fabrics, it is probably easiest to combine like fabrics—cotton with linen, silk with satin and/or velvet. Let your judgment guide you. If you like the way it looks, that's all that matters. If possible, use fabrics that will not easily fray when cut.

If the project is to be washable, check all fabrics to make certain that they are both colorfast and preshrunk. You *can* rely on the manufacturers' labels, but the safest method is to wash all fabrics in very hot water before using them. Be especially wary of reds and dark blues, which tend to bleed if the original dyeing was not done with care. All new washable materials should be washed to remove any sizing.

Cutting the Fabric

Cutting is one of the most important steps in making any kind of patchwork. You must be accurate in order to have the pattern fit perfectly.

Press all fabric to remove wrinkles and crease marks. Check the grain line of the fabric carefully. Lengthwise threads should be parallel to the selvage and crosswise threads exactly perpendicular to the selvage to insure that the pieces will be correctly cut. If the fabric seems off-grain, pull it gently to straighten it. Do this on the true bias in the opposite direction to the off-grain edge. Continue this stretch-

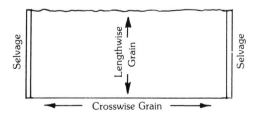

Lengthwise threads should be parallel to the selvage and crosswise threads perpendicular to the selvage.

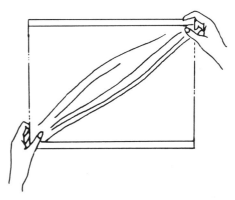

Pull fabric on the true bias in the opposite direction to the off-grain edge to straighten fabric.

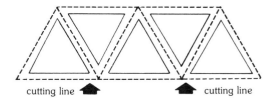

cutting line ◄   ► cutting line

The pieces can share a common cutting line.

ing until the crosswise threads are at right angles to the lengthwise threads.

Lay the fabric on a large, smooth surface with the wrong side up. Have all of your supplies ready: scissors, ruler, sharp pencils and the appropriate templates.

You will notice that the templates include the 1/4″ seam allowance that is traditionally used in quilt making. This seam allowance is especially useful is you are planning to sew your projects on the sewing machine. You can mark off this 1/4″ allowance on the sewing plate of your machine. Then cut your piece with the seam allowance and, by using the marking on your plate, sew with a perfect sewing line. Place the template on the fabric and then trace around the template with a well-sharpened, hard lead pencil; use a light-colored pencil or tailor's chalk for dark fabrics and a regular lead pencil for light fabrics. Hold the pencil at an angle so that the point of the pencil is against the edge of the template.

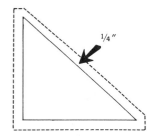

1/4″

The broken line is the cutting line. The solid line is the seam line; match to the line on the next patch. Sewing is done on the solid line.

If you are planning to sew your pieces by hand, you may prefer cutting off the seam allowance on the template. Then trace around the template with the pencil. Now measure 1/4″ around this shape. Using a ruler, draw this second line. This is the line that you will cut on. Now you will see that the first line (where you traced the template) is there to use as a guide for the stitching. The seam allowance does not have to be perfect, but the sewing line must be perfectly straight and true, or the pieces will not fit together into a perfectly shaped design.

You can also combine the two techniques when cutting for hand sewing. First trace around the

template with the seam allowance to give the cutting line. Then cut the seam allowance off the template and lay this smaller template in the center of the cut fabric piece and trace around it to get the sewing line.

Continue moving the template and tracing it on the fabric the required number of times, moving from left to right and always keeping the straight sides parallel with the grain. Try to keep the triangles on the true bias of the fabric by placing the short sides of the triangles on the straight on the fabric. You will conserve fabric by letting pieces share a common cutting line, but if this is confusing leave a narrow border or margin around each piece. A piece of felt placed under the fabric will help to keep it from slipping as you are marking the pieces.

When cutting fabric that is to be used for both strips and blocks, cut the strips first; then cut the patches from the remaining material. Whenever possible, strips should be cut lengthwise along the selvage edge. When necessary, strips may be pieced to get the desired length.

Assembling the Block

It is best to begin by first sewing the pieces into blocks wherever this is indicated in the instructions. Place two pieces together with the right sides facing. Pieces that are to be machine sewn should be carefully placed so that the top edges of both pieces are even. If you are planning to sew by hand, place a pin through both pieces at each end of the sewing line.

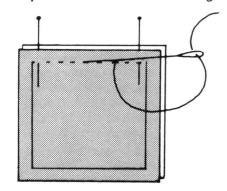

Place a pin through both pieces at each end of the pencil line.

Check on the back to make sure that the pins are exactly on the pencil line. When sewing larger seams, place pins every 1½″, and remove them as you sew past them. Always stitch on the sewing line, being very careful not to stitch into the seam allowance at the corners.

After you join two pieces together, press the seams flat to one side—not open. As a rule, seams should all be pressed in the same direction, but darker pieces

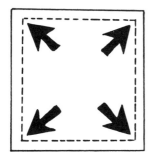

Do not stitch into margins at the corners.

Running stitch.

should not be pressed so that they will fall under the lighter pieces since they may show through when the item is completed. All seams should be pressed before they are crossed with another seam. To keep seams from bunching, clip away excess fabric, if necessary, at these crossing points.

Place the completed block on the ironing board and pull the edges of the block straight with your fingers. After making sure that the block is perfectly square, place pins in the corners and at several places along the edges to hold it rigidly in place. Cover the block with a damp cloth, and steam with a warm iron (or use a steam iron). Do not let the pressing cloth get dry. Iron the edges until they are perfectly square and of equal measurements. The center is ironed last. The block should be ironed perfectly flat with no pucker.

Quilting

Always work from the center out. Otherwise you are apt to end up with a large lump in the middle. The actual quilt stitching is a simple process for any one who can sew. A simple running stitch is used, but it does take a little practice. The stitches should be fairly small and close together.

After using a variety of needles, I recommend the short, fine quilting needle. It allows a rhythm to develop fairly quickly so that the quilting is even and smooth. It is much more difficult to do the running stitch with any speed using a longer needle. But again, use what works best for you. I prefer using No. 50 cotton thread. To begin, make a knot at the end of the thread and bring the needle through to the top of the patchwork, then pull gently but firmly and the knot will slip through the lower layer into the padding, where it will not be seen. To finish off, make a single back stitch and run the thread through the padding. Cut, and the end will be lost. I do not use a frame or hoop when I work on most projects, but this is a matter of personal preference.

Hostess Apron with Three Borders

2. Cut the following for the top border:
One white strip . . . . 24" x 1½"
One white strip . . . . 24" x 1½"
One maroon strip . . . . 26" x 1½"

3. Cut the following for the second border:
Template A . . . . 24 white
Template B . . . . 6 green
Template B . . . . 4 blue
Template B . . . . 2 print

4. Cut the following for the third border:
Template C . . . . 22 print
Template C . . . . 11 lavender
Template C . . . . 11 white
One maroon strip . . . . 26" x 1½"

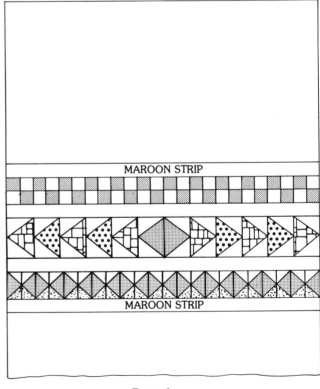

Figure 1

🔲 Print   ▣ Blue
☐ White   ▨ Lavender
🔳 Green

Working the three borders along the bottom of this apron will give you a good introduction into various patchwork techniques. The top border is a variation of Seminole patchwork—in which colorful fabric is sewn into long strips, which are then cut into various shapes and resewn into new strips to create beautiful designs; the middle border is the traditional "Birds in Flight," and the bottom is made with a familiar squares-and-triangles arrangement.

Materials

1½ yards 45"-wide faded-blue homespun cotton polyester; ¼ yard print fabric; ¼ yard maroon fabric; ⅛ yard light-blue fabric; ⅛ yard green fabric; ⅛ yard white fabric; ⅛ yard lavender fabric.

Cutting Directions

1. Cut the following for the apron:
One piece faded-blue . . . . 34" x 27"
Two strips faded-blue . . . . 24" x 4"

Assembly Directions

1. Fold down ¼" along the long sides of the large piece of faded-blue fabric. Press. Turn the same edges under 1″ and stitch down by machine or hand. Press.

2. Fold down ¼″ on the top and bottom. Press. Turn the same edges under 3″. Stitch and press.

3. To form a casing for the belt, make a row of stitching 1″ down from the top of the apron as in figure 2.

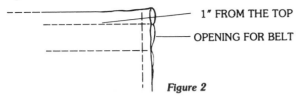

1″ FROM THE TOP

OPENING FOR BELT

Figure 2

4. To make the belt, join the short ends of the two faded-blue strips. Right sides together, fold along the long edge and stitch all the way around, leaving an opening of about 5″. Turn right side out through the opening. Slip stitch the opening. Press.

5. Make the top border:

(a) Sew the white strip and the print strip together along their lengths. Press.

(b) Cut this strip into 1½″ segments as shown in figure 3.

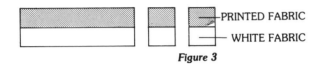

PRINTED FABRIC

WHITE FABRIC

Figure 3

(c) Place the segments next to each other in a checkerboard fashion and sew them together as in figure 4.

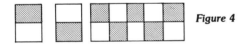

Figure 4

(d) Sew the maroon strip to the checkerboard strip along the length. Press. Turn under along the

long edges and press. Place this top border approximately 10½″ from the bottom of the apron and appliqué in place by hand or machine, using an ornamental stitch if desired. Turn under the raw edges at the sides.

6. Make the second border:

(a) Join two triangles made from Template A to one triangle from Template B to make one segment of the border as shown in figure 5. Sew the segments together, using figure 1 as a guide to

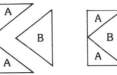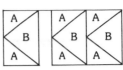

Figure 5

arrangement and color.

(b) Turn under ¼″ along the long seams and press. Appliqué the second border 1″ below the first border by hand or machine, using an ornamental stitch if desired. Turn under the raw edges at the sides.

7. Make the third border:

(a) Sew the triangles together to make a strip, following the layout in figures 1 and 6.

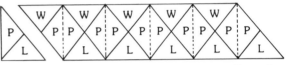

Figure 6

(b) Join the maroon strip to the patchwork strip along the long edge of purple triangles. Press down ¼″ on each of the long edges. Appliqué the third border 1″ below the second border by hand or machine, using an ornamental stitch if desired. Turn under the raw edge at the sides.

8. Thread the belt through the casing, and press the entire apron.

The templates for this project appear on Plate 1.

Pennsylvania Dutch Eyeglass Case

Pennsylvania Dutch quilts were made with bright-colored fabrics of maximum intensity, stitched together in strong, bold designs. This eyeglass case is based upon a traditional Pennsylvania Dutch quilt block and is made with clear, bright Pennsylvania Dutch colors.

Materials

⅛ yard orange fabric; ⅛ yard pink fabric; ⅛ yard blue fabric; ⅛ yard purple fabric; ¼ yard maroon fabric; 7½″ square lightweight batting; 7½″ square interfacing.

Cutting Directions

1. Cut the following for the block:

Template A . . . . 1 orange
Template B . . . . 4 pink
Template C . . . . 4 maroon
Template D . . . . 4 blue
Template D . . . . 4 purple
Template E . . . . 2 maroon
Template F . . . . 2 maroon

2. Cut the following for the lining:

One piece maroon . . . . 7½″ x 7½″

3. Cut the following for the interfacing:

One piece lightweight interfacing . . 7½″ x 7½″

4. Cut the following for the batting:

One piece batting . . . . 7½″ x 7½″

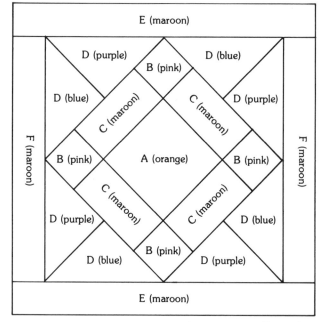

Figure 1

Assembly Directions

1. Following the block diagram in figure 1, assemble the block. Start with the center orange piece made from Template A and attach two maroon

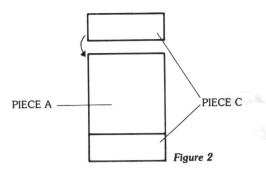

PIECE A

PIECE C

Figure 2

pieces made from Template C. (See figure 2.) Then sew the pink pieces made from Template B to the remaining maroon pieces made from Template C, as in figure 3. Sew these pieces together to form the central block shown in figure 4.

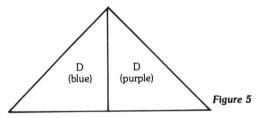

PIECE C

PIECE B

Figure 3

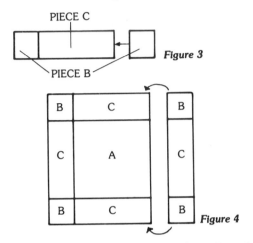

B	C		B
C	A		C
B	C		B

Figure 4

2. Sew the purple triangles made from Template D to the blue triangles made from the same template as shown in figure 5, and join these triangles to the central block to form a large square.

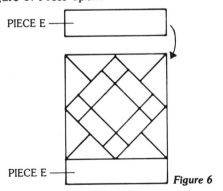

D (blue)   D (purple)

Figure 5

3. Attach the two maroon pieces made from Template E to the top and bottom of the square, as in figure 6. Press open.

PIECE E

PIECE E

Figure 6

4. Attach the two maroon pieces made from Template F to the sides of the rectangle as in figure 7. Press open.

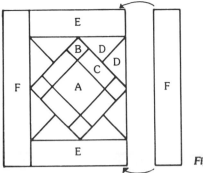

E

B   D
C   D

F   A   F

E

Figure 7

5. Place the batting on the interfacing, and then place the completed block on top of the batting. Pin and baste through all of the thicknesses. Top stitch by hand or machine through all of the thicknesses as shown in figure 8.

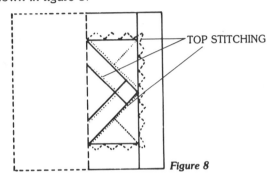

TOP STITCHING

Figure 8

6. Right sides together, join the lining to the finished block and sew across the top and down 2″ along the two sides as shown in figure 9.

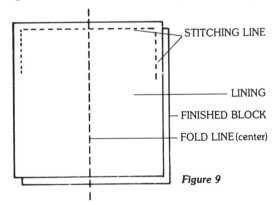

STITCHING LINE

LINING

FINISHED BLOCK

FOLD LINE (center)

Figure 9

7. Lift the lining flap out of the way and fold the block along the fold line indicated in figure 9, with the right sides together. Stitch along the bottom and up the side to where the lining is attached. Fold the lining along the fold line with right sides together, and stitch up the sides to where the lining is attached. *Do not sew along the bottom of the lining.*

8. Clip the corners, and turn the eyeglass case and the lining right side out. Slip-stitch the opening along the bottom of the lining and tuck the lining inside the case. Press the edges lightly with a steam iron.

The templates for this project appear on Plate 2.

Wall Hangings

These two familiar quilt blocks—"The Moon and the Mountain" and "The Variable Star"—are executed here in traditional colors to produce two 12"-square blocks which can be used as complementary wall hangings. The two blocks can be used separately or together, without the borders, to make a quilt.

Materials

1 yard navy blue fabric; 1 yard gold fabric; 1 yard white polka dot with navy background fabric; 1 yard unbleached muslin; two 14" x 14" squares polyester fiber batting. *Note: This yardage will make the two wall hangings.*

MOON AND THE MOUNTAIN

Cutting Directions

1. Cut the following for the block:
    Template C . . . . 1 navy
    Template D . . . . 1 gold
    One piece polka-dotted fabric . . . . . 12" x 12"
2. Cut the following for the borders:
    One navy strip . . . . 68" x 1½"
    One gold strip . . . . 68" x 1"
3. Cut the following for the hangers:
    One strip polka-dotted fabric . . . . . 16" x 4½"
4. Cut the following for the lining:
    One piece unbleached muslin . . . . . 14" x 14"
5. Cut the following for the backing:
    One piece navy . . . . 14½" x 14½"
6. Cut the following for the filling:
    One piece batting . . . . 14" x 14"

Assembly Directions

1. Turn under ¼" on the raw edges of the "moon," made from Template D, and press down. Center the "moon" on the 12" polka-dotted square; pin, baste and appliqué the "moon" in place, using a blind stitch.

2. Turn under the seam allowance on the "mountain," made from Template C, as for the "moon." Baste the tip of the "mountain" over the center of the "moon" and appliqué the "mountain" in place. (See figure 1.)

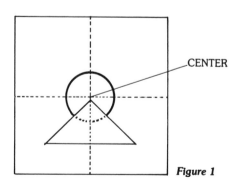

Figure 1

3. Sew the two border strips together along the long edges. Press flat. Apply as a border to the 12" square, placing the gold border strip on the inside. (See figure 2.)

4. Place the muslin square on a flat surface. Place the batting directly on the muslin and place the completed block on top of the batting. Pin and baste through all three thicknesses. Quilt the block follow-

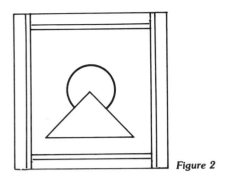

Figure 2

VARIABLE STAR

Cutting Directions

1. Cut the following for the block:

Template A . . . . 4 gold
Template B . . . . 12 gold
Template B . . . . 8 navy
Template B . . . . 4 polka dot

2. Cut the following for the borders:

One navy strip . . . . 68″ x 1½″
One gold strip . . . . .68″ x 1″

3. Cut the following for the hangers:

One strip polka-dotted fabric . . . . . 16″ x 4½″

4. Cut the following for the lining:

One piece unbleached muslin . . . . . 14″ x 14″

5. Cut the following for the backing:

One piece navy . . . . 14½″ x 14½″

6. Cut the following for the filling:

One piece batting . . . . 14″ x 14″

ing figure 3. The quilting is most effective if done ⅛″ to the side of a seam line rather than over the seam.

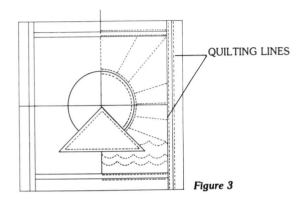

Figure 3

QUILTING LINES

Assembly Directions

1. Following the layout in figure 5, assemble the pieced block.

A (gold)	(gold) B / B (navy)	(gold) B / B (navy)	A (gold)
(navy) B B (gold)	(dot) B B (gold)	(dot) B B (gold)	(navy) B B (gold)
(gold) B / B (navy)	(gold) B B (dot)	(gold) B / B (dot)	(gold) B B (navy)
A (gold)	(navy) B / B (gold)	(navy) B / B (gold)	A (gold)

Figure 5

2. Sew the two border strips together along their long edges. Press flat. Apply as a border, placing the gold border strip on the inside. (See figure 2.)

3. Place the muslin square on a flat surface. Place the batting directly on the muslin and place the completed block on top of the batting. Pin and baste through all three thicknesses. Quilt the block following figure 6.

4. Construct the hangers as described above.

5. Apply the lining as described above.

5. Fold the strip for the hangers lengthwise, with the right side inside, into a long tube. Sew a ¼″ seam and turn right side out. Press flat. Cut this strip into three 5″ pieces and fold each 5″ strip in half. Place one hanger in the center of the block and the other two along the sides 1″ in from the edge as shown in figure 4. Sew each hanger to the block along the seam allowance.

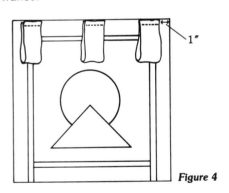

1″

Figure 4

6. With the hangers in the position shown in figure 4, place the backing square on the right side of the block. Pin, baste and sew three of the four edges together. Trim the corners and turn right side out with the hangers projecting upward. Turn in the raw edges and stitch the opening with invisible stitches. Press the finished block lightly to sharpen edges and corners.

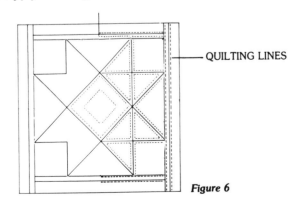

QUILTING LINES

Figure 6

The templates for this project appear on Plates 3, 4 and 5.

Gold Fish—Blue Fish Baby Bibs

The whimsical fish design on these bibs is created with two triangles; the checkerboard center is cleverly constructed of strips which are cut up and rearranged, much in the style of Seminole patchwork.

Materials

½ yard white fabric; ½ yard blue fabric; ¼ yard yellow fabric; ⅛ yard bright-orange fabric; ⅛ yard light-blue fabric; ¼ yard lightweight polyester batting; small amounts of yellow and blue 6-strand embroidery floss. *Note: this yardage will make the two bibs.*

GOLD FISH

Cutting Directions

1. Cut the following for the fish block:

Template A . . . . 2 blue
Template B . . . . 2 blue
Template B . . . . 6 yellow
Template C . . . . 2 bright orange
Template C . . . . 2 white

2. Cut the following for the yoke:

Template D . . . . 1 white

3. Cut the following for the ties:

Template E . . . . 2 white

4. Cut the following for the batting:

1 piece . . . . 8″ x 11″

Assembly Directions

1. Following the diagram in figure 1, sew the strips, made from Template C, together, alternating the colors.

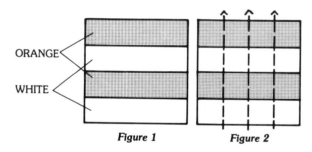

ORANGE
WHITE

Figure 1   *Figure 2*

2. Cut this into strips as shown by the arrows in figure 2.

3. Place the strips as shown in figure 3 to make a checkerboard.

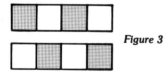

Figure 3

4. Following the layout in figure 4, sew four yellow pieces, made from Template B, to the checkerboard.

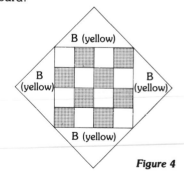

B (yellow)

B (yellow)   B (yellow)

B (yellow)

Figure 4

5. Following the layout in figure 5, sew the remainder of the pieces made from Template B and the pieces made from Template A to the block.

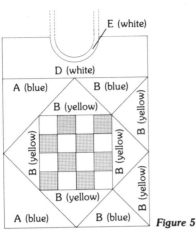

Figure 5

6. Sew the yoke, made from Template D, to the fish block. Press.

7. Place the completed patchwork on top of the batting; baste together and trim away any excess batting.

8. Using the completed bib as a pattern, cut a lining from the white fabric.

9. Right sides together, sew the lining to the completed bib, leaving the neckline open. Clip the corners and turn right side out.

10. Join the two pieces of the ties made from Template E. Press flat. With right sides together, fold in half lengthwise, and leaving an opening that is large enough to accommodate the top of the bib, sew the long sides of the ties. Trim the seam; turn right side out and press. Pin the right side of one edge of the tie opening to the top of the bib. Baste and stitch. Turn under the ¼″ seam allowance on the other side of the tie and slip stitch to the bib.

11. Top stitch through all thicknesses, following the suggestion in figure 6.

12. Embroider the eye and mouth.

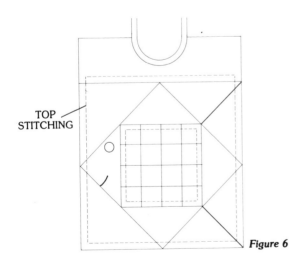

TOP STITCHING

Figure 6

BLUE FISH

Cutting Directions

1. Cut the following for the fish block:

Template A . . . . 2 yellow
Template B . . . . 2 yellow
Template B . . . . 6 blue
Template C . . . . 2 light blue
Template C . . . . 2 white

2. Cut the following for the yoke:

Template D . . . . 1 white

3. Cut the following for the ties:

Template E . . . . 2 white

4. Cut the following for the batting:

1 piece . . . . 8″ x 11″

Assembly Directions

1. Following figure 7, sew the strips, made from Template C, together alternating the colors.

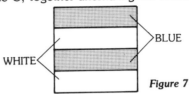

BLUE

WHITE

Figure 7

2. Cut this into strips as shown by the arrows in figure 2.

3. Place the strips as shown in figure 3 to make a checkerboard.

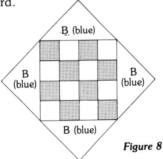

B (blue)

B (blue)   B (blue)

B (blue)

Figure 8

4. Following the layout in figure 8, sew four blue pieces, made from Template B, to the checkerboard.

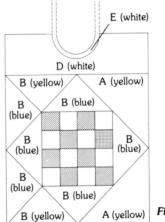

E (white)

D (white)

B (yellow)   A (yellow)

B (blue)   B (blue)

B (blue)   B (blue)

B (blue)   B (blue)

B (blue)   B (blue)

B (yellow)   A (yellow)   *Figure 9*

5. Following the layout in figure 9, sew the remainder of the pieces made from Template B and the pieces made from Template A to the block.

6. Complete as for the Gold Fish bib.

The templates for this project appear in Plates 22, 23 and 24.

Evening Bag

One of the most popular patchwork shapes is the triangle. In this elegant evening bag, triangles are sewn together to form the patchwork square that makes the small purse. The sample in the photograph was made of Qiana® nylon, suitable for evening wear. The bag could also be made in other fabrics.

Materials

½ yard burgundy Qiana® nylon; ⅛ yard rose-pink Qiana® nylon; ⅛ yard white Qiana® nylon; ¼ yard muslin; 17″ x 7½″ piece of lightweight batting; 1½ yards narrow cording; 34″ rhinestone ribbon (optional).

Cutting Directions

1. Cut the following for the blocks:
Template A . . . . 2 burgundy
Template A, reversed . . . . 2 burgundy
Template B . . . . 2 rose-pink
Template B, reversed . . . . 2 rose-pink
Template C . . . . 2 white
Template D . . . . 2 burgundy

2. Cut the following for the backing:
Two pieces muslin . . . . 8½″ x 7½″
3. Cut the following for the batting:
Two pieces lightweight batting . . . . 8½″ x 7½″
4. Cut the following for the lining:
One piece burgundy . . . . 14½″ x 8½″
5. Cut the following for the piping:
One burgundy bias strip . . . . 1½″ x 24″
6. Cut the following for the drawstring:
One burgundy strip . . . . 1¼″ x 24″
7. Cut the following for the shoulder strap:
One burgundy strip . . . . 1¼″ x 34″
One muslin strip . . . . 1¼″ x 34″

Assembly Directions

1. Following the block layout in figure 1, sew together one piece made from Template A, one piece made from Template A, reversed, one piece made from Template B, one piece made from Template B, reversed, and one piece made from Template C to form the block. Repeat for the second block.

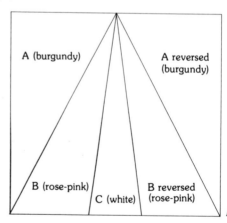

Figure 1

2. Place the batting on the muslin backing, and then place the block on top of the batting, as shown in figure 2. Baste through the three thicknesses. Repeat for the second block.

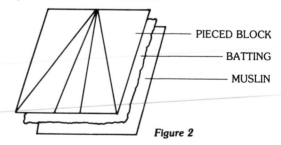

PIECED BLOCK
BATTING
MUSLIN

Figure 2

3. Fold the burgundy bias strip around a 24″ length of cording and sew close to the cording by hand or using the zipper foot on the sewing machine.

4. Apply the cording to one of the blocks as shown in figure 3. Sew in place by hand or using the zipper foot on the sewing machine.

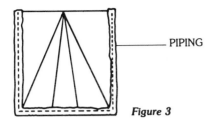

— PIPING

Figure 3

5. Right sides together, pin and sew the blocks together along the three sides of the block that have the cording applied. Sew in place by hand or using the zipper foot on the sewing machine.

6. The casement for the bag is made from the two pieces made from Template D. At either end of one of the pieces made from Template D, fold in 1″ and stitch as show in figure 4.

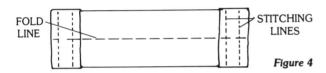

FOLD LINE

STITCHING LINES

Figure 4

7. Fold the piece made from Template D in half lengthwise, and press. Fold under ¼″ on one long side and press down.

8. With the right side of the piece made from Template D facing the inside of the purse, line up the

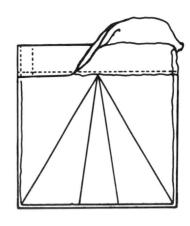

Figure 5

raw edges. Bring down the folded edge over the raw edge of the pouch and top stitch in place. (See figure 5.)

9. Repeat for the second piece made from Template D.

10. Fold the strip for the drawstring in half lengthwise. Sew ¼″ from the edge and turn inside out, making a tube. Draw a 24″ length of cording through this tube. Push the raw edges in at both ends and blind stitch the ends closed. Pass this drawstring through the casement and knot the ends of the string.

11. Baste the muslin interfacing to the wrong side of the shoulder strap. Fold in half, folding under one raw edge and hand stitch.

12. Attach the shoulder strap by hand to the inside of each side of the bag, with small, firm stitches. Use a double thread.

13 (Optional). Hand stitch 34″ of rhinestone ribbon to the side of the shoulder strap that is not seamed, before attaching to the inside of the bag.

The templates for this project appear on Plates 6 and 7.

Crown Jewels Tote Bag

While the "Crown Jewels" patchwork block is the focal point of this tote bag, the bag could be made with any 8″ quilt block. The templates for the block can be used to make a complete "Crown Jewels" quilt.

Materials

⅛ yard red fabric; ⅛ yard white fabric; ⅛ yard gold fabric; ⅛ aqua fabric; ¾ yard red print fabric, which includes the above colors; ¾ yard navy blue wide-wale pique; ¾ yard muslin; ¾ yard lightweight batting; two ¾″ red or navy-blue buttons.

Cutting Directions

1. Cut the following for the blocks:

Template A	2 aqua
Template B	8 white
Template C	8 gold
Template D	8 red
Template E	8 navy
Template E	16 red print

2. Cut the following for the borders:

Four strips navy	2½″ x 8½″
Four strips navy	4½″ x 12½″

3. Cut the following for the lining:

Two pieces red print	12½″ x 16½″

4. Cut the following for the interfacing:

Two pieces muslin	12½″ x 16½″

5. Cut the following for the filling:

Two pieces batting	12½″ x 16½″

6. Cut the following for the shoulder straps:

Two strips red print	2½″ x 22″
Two strips navy	2½″ x 22″
Two strips muslin	2½″ x 22″

Assembly Directions

1. Following the layout in figure 1, construct the block. Begin by sewing the four white pieces made from Template B to the aqua piece made from Template A. Continue in this manner until the four navy pieces made from Template E are attached. Then sew the two red print triangles together and join these to the block.

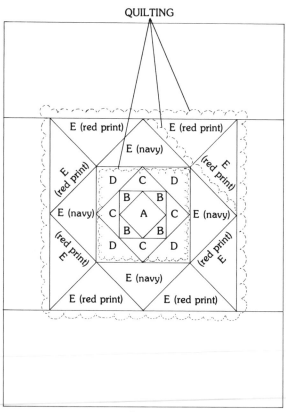

Figure 1

2. Sew the smaller border strips to the sides of the block. Press flat.

3. Sew the larger border strips to the top and bottom of the block. Press flat.

4. Place the batting on top of the muslin interfacing, and then place the completed patchwork on top of the batting. Pin and baste through all thicknesses.

5. Quilt through all thicknesses by hand or machine, following the suggestion in figure 1.

6. Repeat steps 1 through 5 for the second side of the bag.

7. Right sides together, sew the two sides of the bag together with a ¼″ seam along both of the long sides and one short side. Trim the corners and turn the bag right side out. Press lightly with a steam iron.

8. Baste the muslin shoulder strap pieces to the wrong side of the navy shoulder strap pieces. Right sides together, baste the red print shoulder strap pieces to the navy pieces. Sew three sides as shown in figure 2.

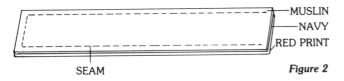

SEAM — — — MUSLIN
— NAVY
RED PRINT

SEAM   *Figure 2*

9. Trim the corners of the strap sections and turn the straps right side out. Press lightly and top stitch ¼″ on three sides of the strap.

10. Make a ⅞″ buttonhole 2″ from the end of one of the straps, and make another buttonhole 4½″ from the end as shown in figure 3.

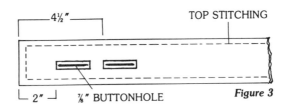

4½″   TOP STITCHING

2″   ⅞″ BUTTONHOLE   *Figure 3*

11. Sew one strap to each side of the bag at the upper left hand corner as shown in figure 4.

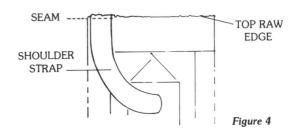

SEAM   TOP RAW EDGE

SHOULDER STRAP

Figure 4

12. Join the red print lining pieces, following the instructions in step 7 for the bag.

13. Press down ½″ along both the top edge of the back and the lining. Insert the lining into the bag, matching the side seams. Pin, baste and blind stitch the lining to the bag with tiny hand stitches. To secure the top and the straps, stitch, by hand or machine, ¼″ from the top through all the thicknesses, working from the outside of the bag.

14. Adjust the shoulder straps to the most comfortable length and sew the two buttons in place. Press the entire bag lightly with a steam iron.

The templates for this project appear on Plate 8.

Crazy Quilt Grow Chart

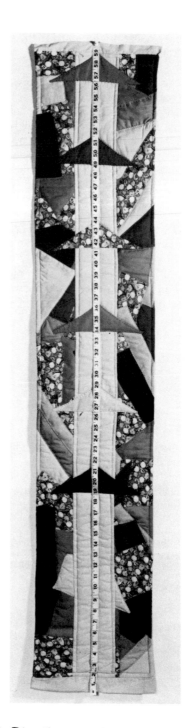

Working on this project will serve as an introduction to another type of quilt: the "crazy quilt." Born of necessity because of the scarcity of fabrics among early quilt makers, the "crazy quilt" used any unworn scraps cut from odd materials. The pieces were sewn together in a "crazy" fashion, usually on an inner lining which held the pieces in place while they were being sewn. Later the lowly crazy quilt was elevated by using only silk and velvet scraps and fastening the pieces with lovely embroidery stitches. These later quilts were not intended as bed coverings, but were used as throws for the Victorian parlor. This adaptation includes a quilted panel which supports a 60″ tape measure, against which a child can stand and have his height determined.

Materials

1½ yards bright-yellow fabric; ⅛ yard orange fabric; ⅛ yard light-green fabric; ⅛ yard dark-green fabric; ⅛ yard bright print fabric, which uses the above colors; 2 yards muslin; lightweight polyester batting (approximately 60″ x 12″); 14″ dowel; 12″ ruler; 60″ tape measure.

Cutting Directions

1. Cut the following for the "crazy" panels:
   One piece muslin . . . . 9″ x 61″
   One piece batting . . . . 9″ x 61″
   Pieces of the various fabrics, cut into squares, rectangles and triangles approximately 5″ long.

2. Cut the following for the center panel:
   One strip yellow . . . . 4½″ x 61″
   One strip muslin . . . . 4½″ x 61″
   One piece batting . . . . 4½″ x 61″

3. Cut the following for the casements:
   One piece yellow . . . . 2½″ x 14″
   One piece yellow . . . . 4″ x 14″

4. Cut the following for the lining:
   One piece muslin . . . . 12½″ x 61″
   (piece if necessary)

5. Cut the following for the arrowheads:
   Template A . . . . 1 yellow
   Template A . . . . 2 orange
   Template A . . . . 1 light green
   Template A . . . . 1 dark green
   Template A . . . . 1 print

Assembly Directions

1. Baste the muslin piece and the batting piece for the "crazy" panels together.

2. With the batting side facing you, place a piece of colored cotton in one corner of the panel. Pin in place. (See figure 1.)

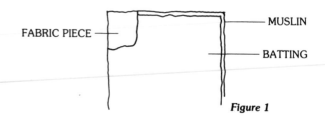

FABRIC PIECE — MUSLIN — BATTING

Figure 1

3. Take a contrasting cotton piece and place it over a raw edge of the first piece, turning under the raw edge of the second piece by ¼″. Pin in place. Take a third piece and pin it over the raw edge of the second, folding the top piece under by ¼″. When you have covered about 9″ in this manner, secure the seams by going over them with a feather stitch. This can be done by hand or with a sewing machine equipped with special embroidery attachments. Cover the entire panel in this manner.

4. Fold the completed panel in half lengthwise and cut along the fold. Baste around the four sides of the panels, ¼″ from the raw edge.

5. Place the batting for the center panel on the corresponding muslin, and then place the yellow strip on top of the batting. Baste through all thicknesses and around the four sides of the panel. Top stitch, by hand or machine, down the center and ⅜″ along either side of the center seam as shown in figure 2.

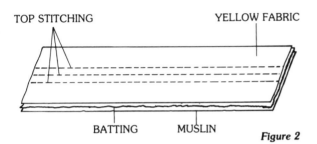

TOP STITCHING YELLOW FABRIC

BATTING MUSLIN

Figure 2

6. Join a "crazy" panel to each side of the center panel.

7. Fold the edges of one of the casement strips in 1″ at either end and stitch in place. Fold lengthwise as shown in figure 3. Repeat for the other strip.

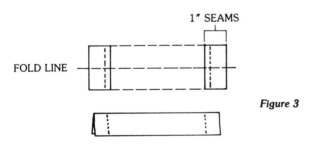

1″ SEAMS

FOLD LINE

Figure 3

8. Sew the casement strips to the right side of the Grow Chart as shown in figure 4, placing the wider strip at the bottom.

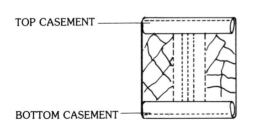

TOP CASEMENT

BOTTOM CASEMENT

Figure 4

9. Fold under ¼″ along each side of the arrowheads made from Template A. Place the tip of the first arrowhead along the center line flush with the top casement seam. Pin in place and sew by hand or machine, using a feather stitch if desired. Continue adding the rest of the arrowheads, placing them 7½″ from the tip of the previous one. (See figure 5.)

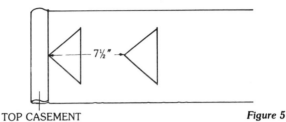

←—7½″—→

TOP CASEMENT *Figure 5*

10. Place the muslin lining on the right side of the panel, with the casement flaps turned inward. Pin and sew three sides. Trim corners and turn right side out. Slip stitch the opening. Top stitch through all thicknesses as shown in figure 6.

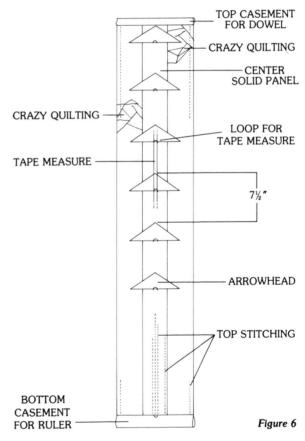

TOP CASEMENT FOR DOWEL

CRAZY QUILTING

CENTER SOLID PANEL

CRAZY QUILTING

LOOP FOR TAPE MEASURE

TAPE MEASURE

7½″

ARROWHEAD

TOP STITCHING

BOTTOM CASEMENT FOR RULER

Figure 6

11. Place the tape measure so that the beginning of the tape is at the bottom of the Grow Chart and the end is at the top. Secure the tape at the top by machine or hand. Make a series of loops with sewing or embroidery thread at the points indicated in figure 6.

12. Insert the dowel through the top casement and the ruler through the bottom casement.

The templates for this project appear on Plate 9.

Basket of Flowers Placemats, Napkins and Centerpiece

One the most popular patchwork techniques is the clever arrangement of squares, triangles and rectangles to make a basket. In this project, the basket is filled with "flowers," also made of patchwork pieces.

Materials

2½ yards floral print fabric; ⅛ yard green fabric; ⅛ yard lavender fabric; ½ yard pink fabric; ½ yard yellow fabric; ¼ yard off-white fabric; 2 yards muslin, cotton or pellon (for interfacing). *Note: This yardage will make four placemats, four napkins and one centerpiece.*

PLACEMAT

Note: These instructions are for one placemat; repeat for the other three.

Cutting Directions

1. Cut the following for the block:

Template A	1 off-white
Template A, reversed	1 off-white
Template B	2 green
Template C	2 green
Template D	1 yellow
Template E	1 yellow
Template F	2 off-white
Template G	4 floral print
Template H	1 lavender
Template H	2 pink
Template I	1 off-white
Template I, reversed	1 off-white

2. Cut the following for the borders:

Two strips yellow	8½″ x 2″
Two strips floral print	13″ x 5¾″

3. Cut the following for the backing:
   One piece floral print . . . . .19″x 13″
4. Cut the following for the interfacing:
   One piece interfacing . . . . 19″ x 13″

Assembly Directions

1. Working on a flat surface, take all of the pieces that have been cut out for the block and orient them as they appear in figure 1 to produce the design.

2. Assemble the block by starting in the lower left hand corner with the off-white piece from Template A and attach it the green piece from Template B. This makes the first section. Put it aside.

3. Following the arrows, attach the green piece from Template C to the yellow piece made from

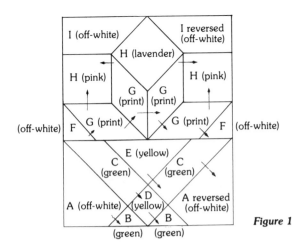

I (off-white)   I reversed (off-white)
H (lavender)
H (pink)   H (pink)
G (print)   G (print)
(off-white) F   G (print)   G (print)   F (off-white)
E (yellow)
C (green)   C (green)
A (off-white)   D (yellow)   A reversed (off-white)
B (green)   B (green)

Figure 1

Template D to the green piece made from Template B. Sew this strip to the first section made in step 2.

4. Following the arrows, attach the yellow piece made from Template E to the green piece made from Template C to the off-white piece made from Template A, reversed. Sew this strip to the previously assembled sections, and the "basket" portion of the design is completed. Put this aside.

5. Following the arrows in figure 1, assemble the "flowers" portion of the design.

6. Sew the "flowers" to the "basket" in one straight seam.

7. Add the yellow borders to the top and bottom of the block, and add the floral borders to the sides. (See figure 2.)

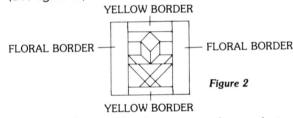

YELLOW BORDER
FLORAL BORDER —   — FLORAL BORDER
YELLOW BORDER

Figure 2

8. Place this completed piece over the interfacing and baste in place.

9. With right sides together, place the backing over the completed block and stitch through all three thicknesses with a ½" seam along three sides as shown in figure 3.

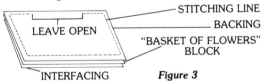

STITCHING LINE
LEAVE OPEN — BACKING
"BASKET OF FLOWERS" BLOCK
INTERFACING   *Figure 3*

10. Turn the placemat right side out. Slip stitch the opening. Iron to flatten the edges and corners.

11. Run two rows of ornamental top stitching through thicknesses as shown in figure 4. Either machine or hand stitching may be used.

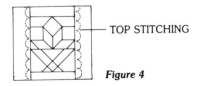

— TOP STITCHING

Figure 4

NAPKINS

Cutting Directions

1. Cut the following for four napkins:
    Two squares yellow . . . . 17" x 17"
    Two squares pink . . . . 17" x 17"

Assembly Directions

1. Turn under ¼" along the raw edges. Press and turn under ¼" again.

2. Stitch close to the fold and press.

CENTERPIECE

Cutting Directions

1. Cut the following for the blocks:
    Template A . . . . 2 off-white
    Template A, reversed . . . . 2 off-white
    Template B . . . . 4 green
    Template C . . . . 4 green
    Template D . . . . 2 yellow
    Template E . . . . 2 yellow
    Template F . . . . 4 off-white
    Template G . . . . 8 floral print
    Template H . . . . 2 lavender
    Template H . . . . 4 pink
    Template I . . . . 2 off-white
    Template I, reversed . . . . 2 off-white

2. Cut the following for the borders:
    One strip yellow . . . . 8½" x 2"
    Two pieces floral print . . . . 24" x 4½"

3. Cut the following for the backing:
    One piece floral print . . . . 24" x 16"

4. Cut the following for the interfacing:
    One piece interfacing . . . . 24" x 16"

Assembly Directions

1. Assemble two blocks, following steps 1-6 under the instructions for the placemat.

2. Add the yellow borders to the top and bottom of one block and only to the top of the second block.

3. Orient the blocks as shown in figure 5 and join the two blocks.

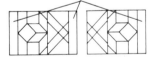

YELLOW BORDER

Figure 5

4. Add the floral borders to the long sides of the blocks as shown in figure 6.

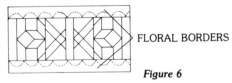

FLORAL BORDERS

Figure 6

5. Place this completed piece over the interfacing and baste in place.

6. With right sides together, place the backing over the completed block and finish as for the placemats.

7. Run two rows of ornamental top stitching through all thicknesses as shown in figure 6.

The templates for this project appear on Plates 10 and 11.

Drunkard's Path Pillow

The "Drunkard's Path" is one of the many variations that can be made from the use of just the two patchwork shapes given here. By using different colors and arranging the blocks in various combinations, any number of designs can be created. Some pattern names, such as "Drunkard's Path", which describes the faltering steps of someone in his cups, give a clear picture of a situation; others, such as "Fool's Puzzle" or "Harvest Moon" are less descriptive.

Materials

¼ yard floral print fabric with white background; ¼ yard red fabric; 1½ yards white fabric; 12″ square pillow form or 12″ x 24″ gauze-wrapped polyester batting; 12″ square muslin; 12″ square light-weight polyester batting.

Cutting Directions

1. Cut the following for the block:

Template A . . . . 8 floral print
Template A . . . . 8 red
Template B . . . . 8 floral print
Template B . . . . 8 red

2. Cut the following for the ruffle:

Template C . . . . 10 white

3. Cut the following for the backing:

One piece white . . . . 12″ x 12″

Assembly Directions

1. Sew the floral print pieces made from Template A to the red pieces made from Template B. Sew the red pieces made from Template A to the floral print pieces made from Template B. With the right sides together, place the "B" piece on the "A" piece, as shown in figure 1. Place the center of curve "B" on

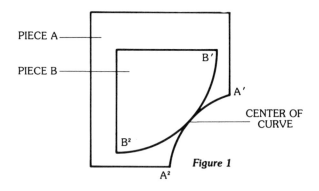

PIECE A
PIECE B
B′
A′
CENTER OF CURVE
B²
A²
Figure 1

the center of curve "A" and pin. Now pin B¹ to A¹ and B² to A² as shown on figure 2. Adjust and pin the fullness of the curves. Baste and stitch ¼″ away from the raw edges. Press the square flat. Eight squares will look like figure 2 and eight squares will look like figure 3.

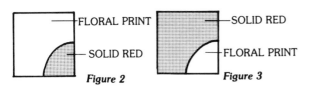

FLORAL PRINT
SOLID RED

Figure 2

SOLID RED
FLORAL PRINT

Figure 3

2. Following the block diagram in figure 4, and working on a flat surface, arrange all of the pieces as they appear in the diagram.

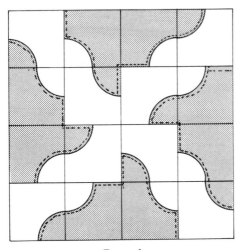

Figure 4

☐ FLORAL PRINT
▦ SOLID RED

3. Place the 12″-square lightweight polyester batting on the 12″-square muslin. Place the completed "Drunkard's Path" block on top of the batting and baste through all three thicknesses.

4. Quilt along the solid red, ¼″ away from the seam line, outlining the four arms of the "Drunkard's Path" design.

5. To make the ruffle, join five of the pieces made from Template C along the notched edge, leaving one end open. Repeat for the other five pieces. Press the seams open.

6. With right sides together, join the long, curved edge of the ruffle (See figure 5). Notch the curve every ¾″, and turn right side out. Press.

Figure 5

7. Using a contrasting thread, run a row of ornamental topstitching ¼″ from the edge of the ruffle. Stitch the raw edges together close to the raw edge, and clip the curve every inch. (See figure 6.)

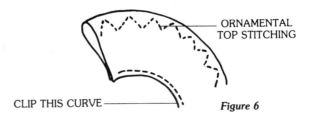

ORNAMENTAL TOP STITCHING

CLIP THIS CURVE

Figure 6

8. With right sides together, place the ruffle on the raw edges of the quilted "Drunkard's Path" block and sew it in place, clipping the corners to make a sharp turn. Sew all around. Join the raw edges of the ruffle, cutting off excess if necessary. (See figure 7.)

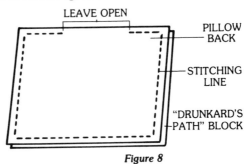

STITCHING LINE

CLIP THIS CORNER

RUFFLE

"DRUNKARD'S PATH" BLOCK
(right side)

Figure 7

9. With right sides together, place the backing on top of the finished block with the applied ruffle turned toward the center of the block so as not to be caught in the final seaming. Sew three sides of the block as shown in figure 8.

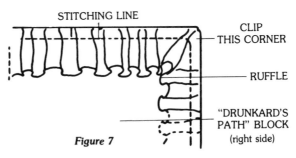

LEAVE OPEN

PILLOW BACK

STITCHING LINE

"DRUNKARD'S PATH" BLOCK

Figure 8

10. Clip the corners and turn the pillow inside out. Insert the 12″ pillow form, or the batting which has been folded to a 12″ square, and close the opening by hand.

The templates for this project appear on Plates 12 and 13.

Baby Blocks Floor Pillow

This delightful plump pillow is based upon the "Baby Blocks" quilt design, a design which is actually an optical illusion. As you stare at the completed patchwork, the eye finds many different forms, and the pattern changes first one way and then another. The startling part about this optical illusion is that the pattern is actually made with only one main pattern piece: a diamond.

Materials

(Note: Corduroy or velvet fabrics are best.) ¼ yard pink fabric; ¼ yard tan fabric; ¼ yard orange fabric; ¼ yard burnt-sienna fabric; ½ yard deep-orange fabric; 1 yard dark-brown fabric; 1 yard muslin; ⅓ yard lightweight polyester batting; 1 yard 3″ polyester batting (or shredded foam).

Cutting Directions

1. Cut the following for the pillow:

Template A . . . . 7 pink
Template A . . . . 7 tan
Template A . . . . 7 orange
Template A . . . . 7 burnt sienna
Template A . . . . 14 deep orange
Template A . . . . 24 dark brown
Template B . . . . 6 dark brown

Template C . . . . 6 dark brown
Template D . . . . 4 tan
Template D . . . . 4 orange
Template D . . . . 4 deep orange
Template E . . . . 4 deep orange
Template E . . . . 2 orange
Template E . . . . 2 burnt sienna
Template E . . . . 2 tan
Template E . . . . 2 pink
Template D . . . . 6 polyester batting
Template E . . . . 6 polyester batting

Assembly Directions

1. Following figure 1, assemble six of the lighter pieces made from Template A to form a six pointed star.

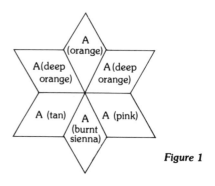

Figure 1

2. Attach six dark brown pieces made from Template A as shown in figure 2. This will become the center star.

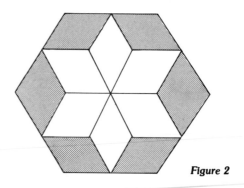

Figure 2

3. Make six more stars following the directions in step 1. Add one brown diamond made from Template A to each of these stars, following figure 3.

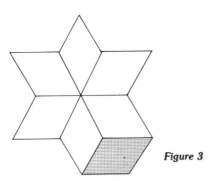

Figure 3

4. Join the six stars around the center star following the layout in figure 4.

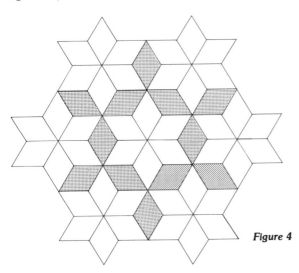

Figure 4

5. Construct six units as shown in figure 5, using for each two brown diamonds made from Template A and one brown triangle made from Template B.

A (dark brown) B (dark brown) A (dark brown)

Figure 5

6. Sew these units between the spaces made by the outer edge of two stars around the center star as shown in figure 6.

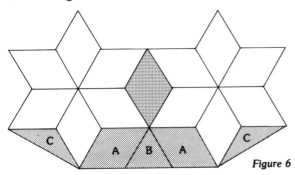

Figure 6

7. Sew six brown pieces made from Template C in position as shown in figure 6 to complete the outer edge of the stars.

8. Right sides together, sew two of the same color pieces made from Template D along two sides. Pin a piece of batting made from Template D to the wrong side, as shown in figure 7, and sew through all thicknesses along two sides of the triangle. Turn right sides out and press the piece. Baste the open side.

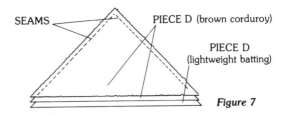

SEAMS PIECE D (brown corduroy)

PIECE D (lightweight batting)

Figure 7

9. Construct the other five pairs made from Piece D in a similar fashion.

10. Construct the six pairs of triangles, made from Piece E, following the directions in step 8.

11. Following the layout in figure 8, baste the triangles just constructed to the right side of the pieced pillow. Sew in place.

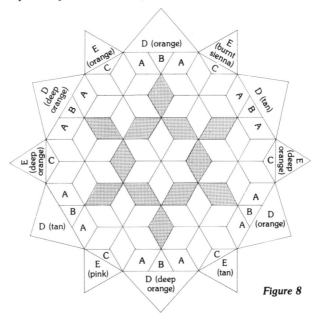

Figure 8

12. Before extending the points, as in the finished pillow, trace the outline of the pillow carefully on a large piece of paper. Using this as a guide, cut out a piece of brown corduroy for the back of the pillow. At the same time, cut two pieces of muslin to make the pillow insert.

13. With the border points facing the center of the right side of the pieced pillow and with right sides together, fit the back to the pillow, carefully matching the shape. Sew in place, leaving a 10″-opening.

14. Sew the two pieces of muslin together, leaving an opening. Turn the muslin form inside out. Stuff evenly with the deep polyester batting or shredded foam. Slip stitch the opening.

15. Turn the corduroy pillow inside out, and gently pull the points to shape the pillow. Insert the muslin pillow form into the corduroy pillow. Adjust the fullness of the insert to the shape of the pillow. Slip stitch the opening.

The templates for this project appear on Plates 18 and 19.

Carpenter's Wheel Sofa Throw

Trades and occupations of the nineteenth century were a great source of inspiration for quilt names such as the "Carpenter's Wheel." Curiously, this quilt pattern gives a feeling of a round wheel although it is constructed with no circular pieces! Shown here as a small sofa throw, the project could also be used as a wall hanging. Several of the blocks pieced together would make a most attractive quilt.

Materials

1 yard gray-green velour; ½ yard maroon velour; ½ yard eggshell suedecloth; 2½ yards gray-green satin lining fabric; 1¼ yards muslin; 40″ square deep polyester batting.

Cutting Directions

1. Cut the following for the block:
    Template A . . . . 16 gray-green
    Template B . . . . 16 maroon
    Template B . . . . 16 eggshell
    Template C . . . . 16 gray-green
2. Cut the following for the first border:
    Two gray-green strips . . . . 6″ x 24″
    Two gray-green strips . . . . 6″ x 34″
3. Cut the following for the second border:
    Template B . . . . 4 maroon
    Template B . . . . 4 eggshell
    Four gray-green strips . . . . 3″ x 31½″
4. Cut the following for the filling:
    Polyester batting . . . . 40″ x 40″
5. Cut the following for the backing:
    One piece muslin . . . . 40″ x 40″

Assembly Directions

1. Following the diagram in figure 1, which is a detail of one-quarter of the block, construct the

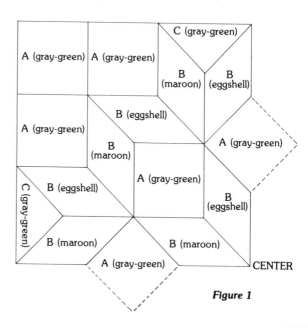

Figure 1

block. Start at the center with the eggshell diamond made from Template B, and work outward in the colors indicated. Construct four quarters. Assemble two quarters to each other and repeat with the other two quarters. Join the halves to complete the block, adjusting the halves carefully so that the motif lies flat. Be especially careful to orient the quarters so that the completed design follows figure 2.

2. Sew the two shorter strips of the first border to the top and bottom of the block. Flatten and steam press.

3. Sew the two longer strips of the first border to the sides of the block. Flatten and steam press.

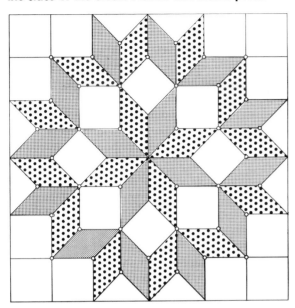

Figure 2

☐ GRAY-GREEN
▨ MAROON
▣ EGGSHELL

4. Place one of the remaining pieces made from Template B on the ends of each of the strips to be used for the second border, as shown in figure 3. Mark with chalk and cut away the excess.

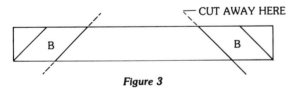

Figure 3

5. Sew a maroon and an eggshell piece made from Template B onto the end of each border strip as shown in figure 4.

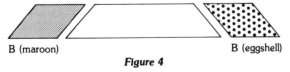

B (maroon)   B (eggshell)

Figure 4

6. Sew the second borders to each of the four sides as shown in figure 5.

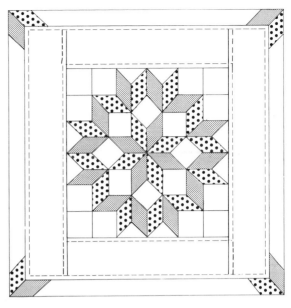

Figure 5

☐ GRAY-GREEN)
▨ MAROON
▣ EGGSHELL

7. Place the batting on the muslin backing, and then place the completed patchwork on top of the batting. Pin and baste through all of the thicknesses.

8. Cut the fabric for the lining in half, crosswise, and sew the two lengths together at the selvage.

9. Place the right side of the lining piece on the right side of the patchwork, aligning the center seam of the lining with the center of the wheel motif. Pin and baste in place, cutting away any excess lining fabric.

10. Sew three sides together, ½″ from the edge. Turn inside out and blind stitch the open end with small, invisible stitches.

11. Quilt around the eggshell pieces made from Template B, ½″ from the seam line.

12. Quilt around the first border, ¼″ from the seam line, as shown by the broken lines in figure 5.

13. Tack through all thicknesses at the points indicated with circles on figure 2. This can be done by hand or machine, with the stitch setting at 0 or 1.

The templates for this project appear on Plates 20 and 21.

Sunburst Kitchen Combination

POTHOLDERS

Cutting Directions

1. Cut the following pieces for the block:

Template A . . . . 8 blue
Template B . . . . 8 deep yellow
Template C . . . . 2 white
Template D . . . . 2 deep orange
Template E . . . . 16 brown print

2. Cut the following for the borders:

Two strips deep yellow . . . . 6½″ x 1½″
Two strips deep yellow . . . . 8½″ x 1½″

3. Cut the following for the lining:

Two pieces unbleached muslin . . . . . . 8″ x 8″

4. Cut the following for the backing:

Two pieces brown print . . . . 8″ x 8″

5. Cut the following for the filling:

Two pieces batting . . . . 8″ x 8″

6. Cut the following for the loop:

Template F . . . . 2 brown print

Assembly Directions

Note: The instructions given here are for one potholder. Repeat procedures for the second.

1. Following the layout in figure 1, assemble the block. Sew the blue and yellow diamonds together first to form a star; then add the print triangles between the points of the star.

The "Sunburst," a very old but extremely popular quilt pattern serves as the basis for this kitchen combination, which includes a pair of potholders and a toaster cover. The sides of the toaster cover are constructed through another method of quilt making called "strip" or "string" quilting. The individual block used to make the potholders could be used to make an entire quilt.

Materials

1 yard brown print fabric; 1 yard unbleached muslin; ⅛ yard deep-orange fabric; ⅛ yard white fabric; ⅛ yard blue fabric; ½ yard deep-yellow fabric; ½ yard polyester batting. *Note: This yardage will make a toaster cover to fit a standard toaster and two potholders.*

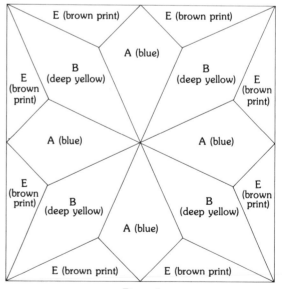

Figure 1

2. Apply the borders as shown in figure 2 and press flat.

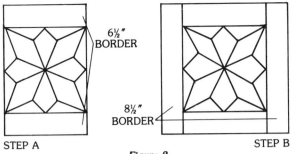

6½″
BORDER

8½″
BORDER

STEP A

STEP B

Figure 2

3. Place the batting over the muslin lining. Place the pieced suburst block over the batting and lining and baste through all the thicknesses.

4. Fold down the seam allowances of the pieces made from Templates C and D. Press. Pin, baste and appliqué them as shown in figure 3. The orange square should be appliquéd on top of the white square.

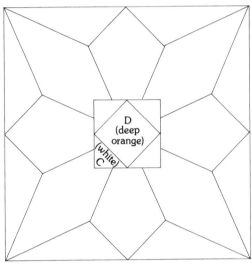

D
(deep orange)

(white)
C

Figure 3

5. Quilt the inside of the deep yellow star following figure 4.

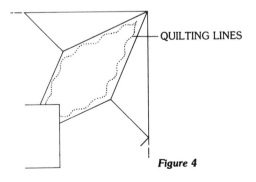

QUILTING LINES

Figure 4

6. Fold the piece made from Template F in half lengthwise, with the right sides together. Stitch along the length and turn right side out to make the potholder loop. Fold the loop in half and secure to the corner of the block as shown in figure 5.

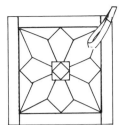

Figure 5

7. With right sides together, place the backing square over the "Sunburst" block and sew three of the four sides along the ¼″ seam allowance.

8. Turn the right sides outside and sew the remaining opening by hand, turning in the raw edges. Press the edges lightly. Run a row of stitches on the border seam through all thicknesses as shown in figure 6.

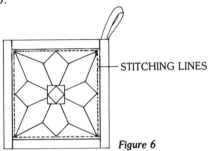

STITCHING LINES

Figure 6

TOASTER COVER

Cutting Directions

Note: Tape pieces of Template H together along edges, matching H¹ and H² before cutting fabric.

1. Cut the following for the toaster cover sides:

Template A	8 blue
Template B	8 deep yellow
Template C	2 white
Template D	2 deep orange
Template G	2 brown print

2. Cut the following for the toaster cover top and ends:

One strip deep orange	25″ x 2″
One strip deep yellow	25″ x 2″
One strip white	25″ x 2″
One strip blue	25″ x 2″

3. Cut the following for the lining and the backing:

Template G	4 muslin
Template H	2 muslin

4. Cut the following for the filling:

Template G	2 batting
Template H	1 batting

Assembly Directions

1. Following the block layout in figure 1, join the yellow diamonds made from Template B to the blue diamonds made from Template A. *Do not add the brown print triangles made from Template E.*

2. Appliqué the pieces made from Templates C and D, following step 4 under the assembly directions for the potholders.

3. Turn under the seam allowances of the "Sunburst" and press.

4. Center the "Sunburst" on the brown print piece made from Template G and appliqué in place. The appliquéing may be done by hand or machine, using the feather stitch of the zigzag sewing machine.

5. Place the batting cut from Template G over the muslin lining cut from Template G. Place the appliquéd "Sunburst" over the batting and lining, and baste through all the thicknesses.

6. Quilt the inside of the deep yellow star as for the potholder, following figure 4.

7. Sew an additional row of straight stitching ¼″ away from the "Sunburst," outlining the whole motif, as shown in figure 7. Repeat for the second side.

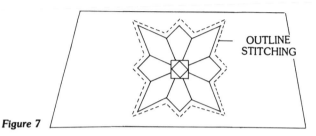

OUTLINE STITCHING

Figure 7

8. To make the top and the ends, place the batting cut from Template H over the muslin lining, cut from Template H. Place the blue strip in place as shown in figure 8 and baste as shown. Place the white strip over the blue strip and sew as shown in figure 9. Turn the white strip over the raw edges of the blue

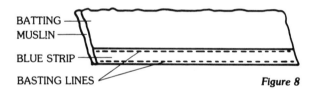

BATTING
MUSLIN
BLUE STRIP
BASTING LINES
Figure 8

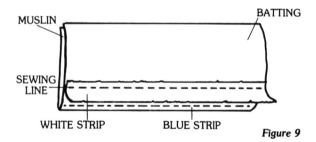

MUSLIN
BATTING
SEWING LINE
WHITE STRIP   BLUE STRIP
Figure 9

strip; flatten the strip and baste down as shown in figure 10. Follow this procedure with the deep yellow and the deep orange strips until the batting is covered with the four colors. This is called "strip" or "string" quilting.

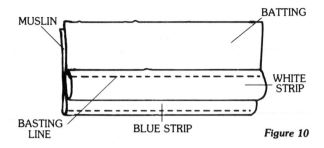

MUSLIN
BATTING
WHITE STRIP
BASTING LINE
BLUE STRIP
Figure 10

9. Sew the sides of the toaster cover to the strip-quilted top, clipping the corners, which are indicated by notches on Template H.

10. Make the backing by sewing the sides of the muslin backing, made from Template G, to the muslin backing, made from Template H, following the procedure in step 8. Leave the seam open between the notches on one side of the top, as shown in figure 11.

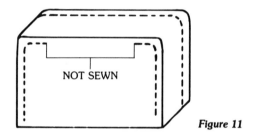

NOT SEWN
Figure 11

11. With right sides together, place the backing over the quilted toaster cover and sew the lower edge all the way around.

12. Turn the cover inside out through the opening in the backing and bring right side out. Slip stitch the opening. On the outside, top stitch—by machine or hand—½″ from the bottom edge of the cover through all of the thicknesses.

The templates for this project appear on Plates 14, 15, 16 and 17.

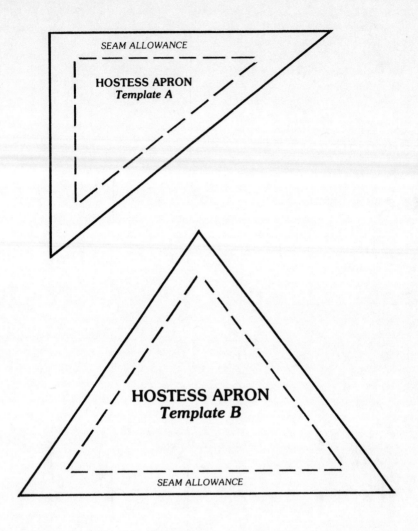

HOSTESS APRON
Template B

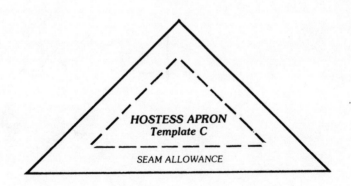

PLATE 1

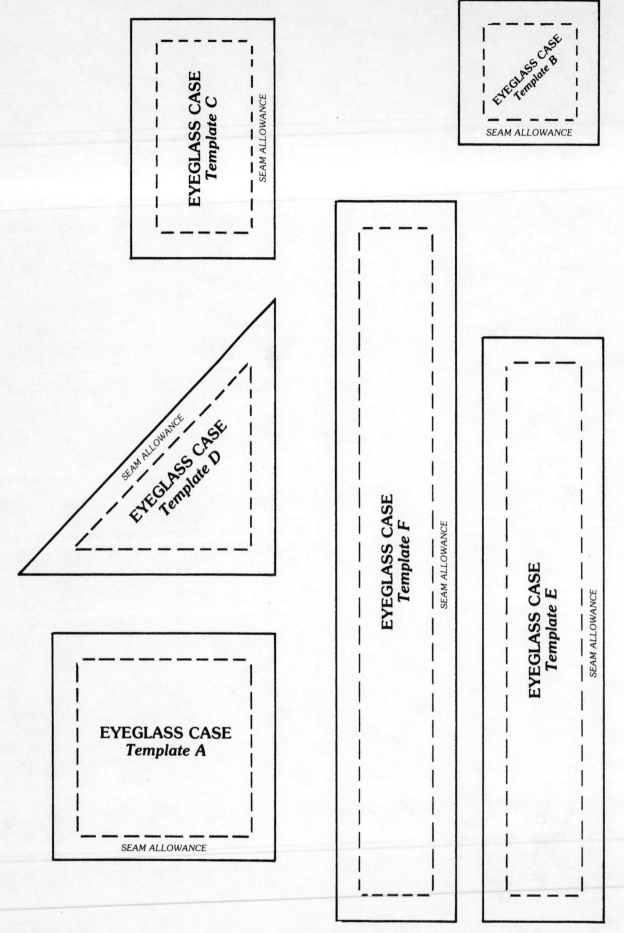

EYEGLASS CASE
Template C
SEAM ALLOWANCE

EYEGLASS CASE
Template B
SEAM ALLOWANCE

SEAM ALLOWANCE
EYEGLASS CASE
Template D

EYEGLASS CASE
Template F
SEAM ALLOWANCE

EYEGLASS CASE
Template E
SEAM ALLOWANCE

EYEGLASS CASE
Template A
SEAM ALLOWANCE

PLATE 2

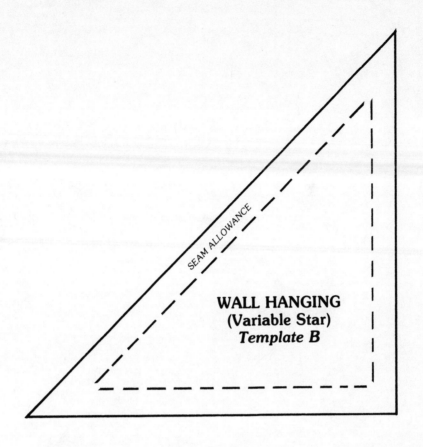

WALL HANGING
(Variable Star)
Template B

SEAM ALLOWANCE

WALL HANGING
(Variable Star)
Template A

SEAM ALLOWANCE

PLATE 3

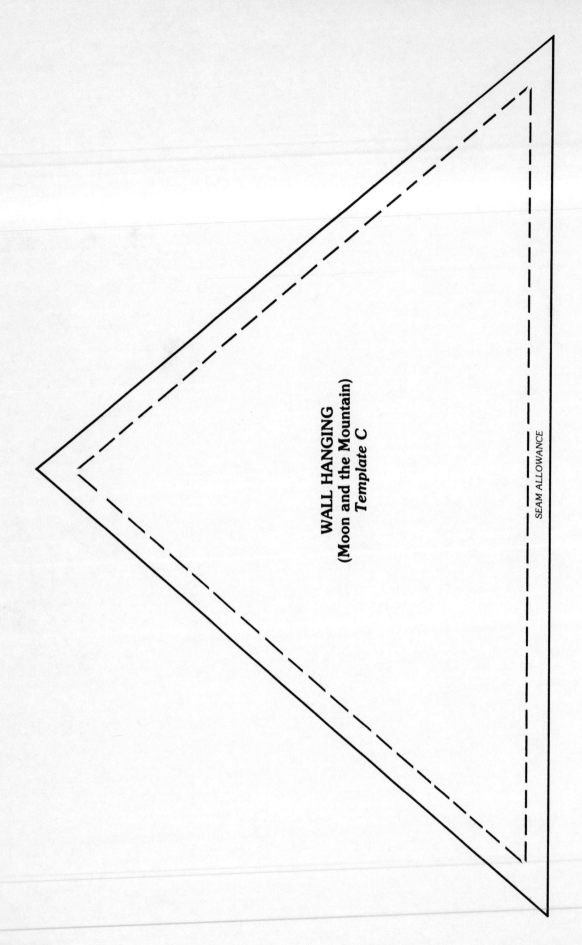

WALL HANGING
(Moon and the Mountain)
Template C

SEAM ALLOWANCE

PLATE 4

WALL HANGING
(Moon and the Mountain)
Template D

SEAM ALLOWANCE

PLATE 5

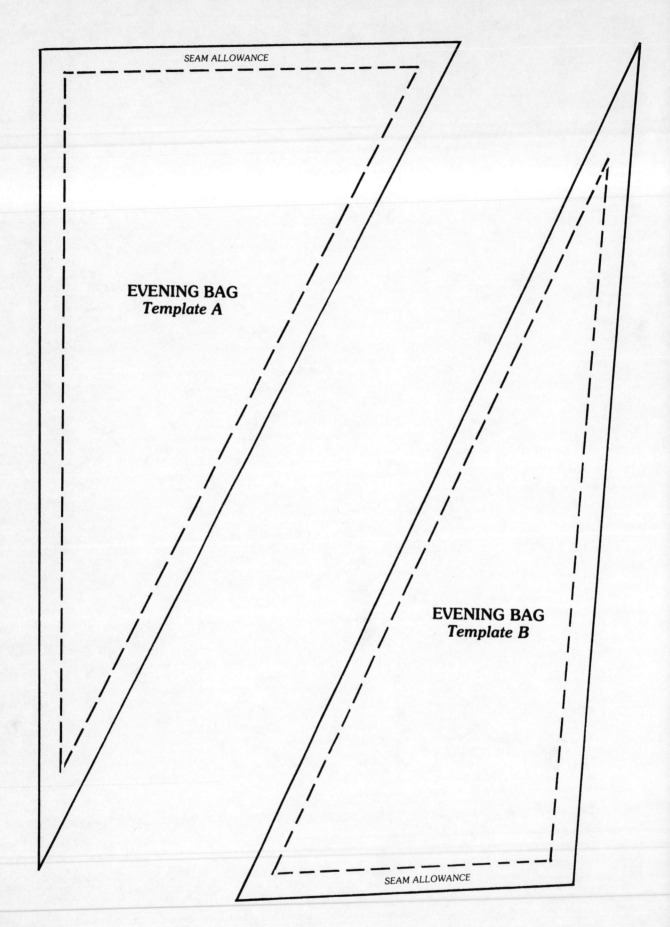

SEAM ALLOWANCE

EVENING BAG
Template A

EVENING BAG
Template B

SEAM ALLOWANCE

PLATE 6

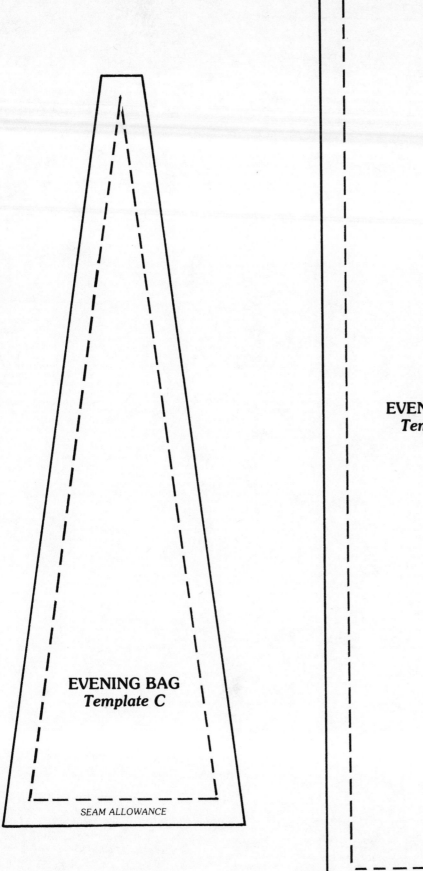

EVENING BAG
Template C

SEAM ALLOWANCE

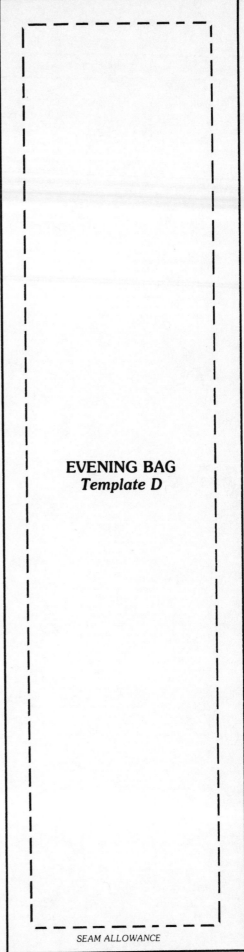

EVENING BAG
Template D

SEAM ALLOWANCE

PLATE 7

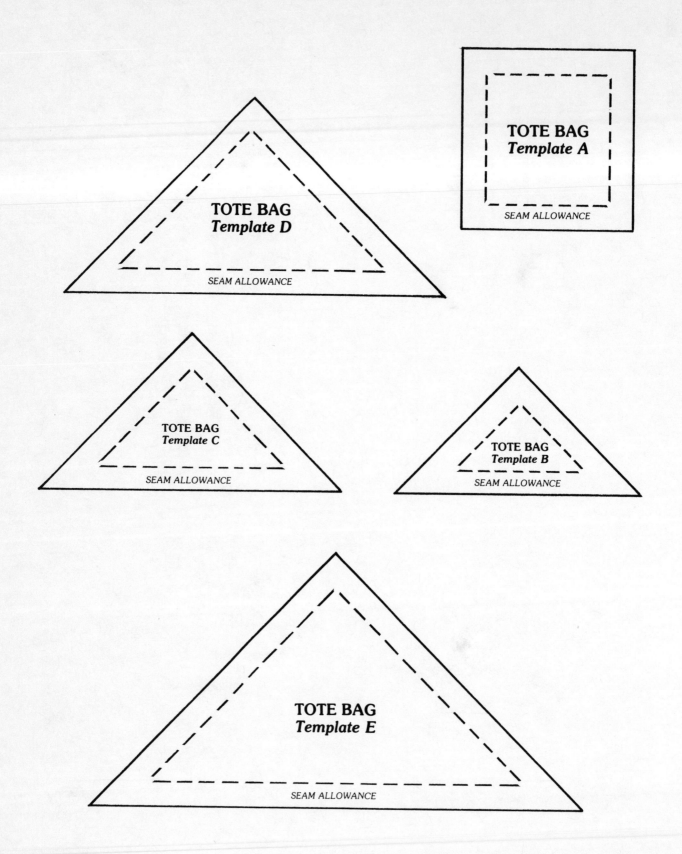

PLATE 8

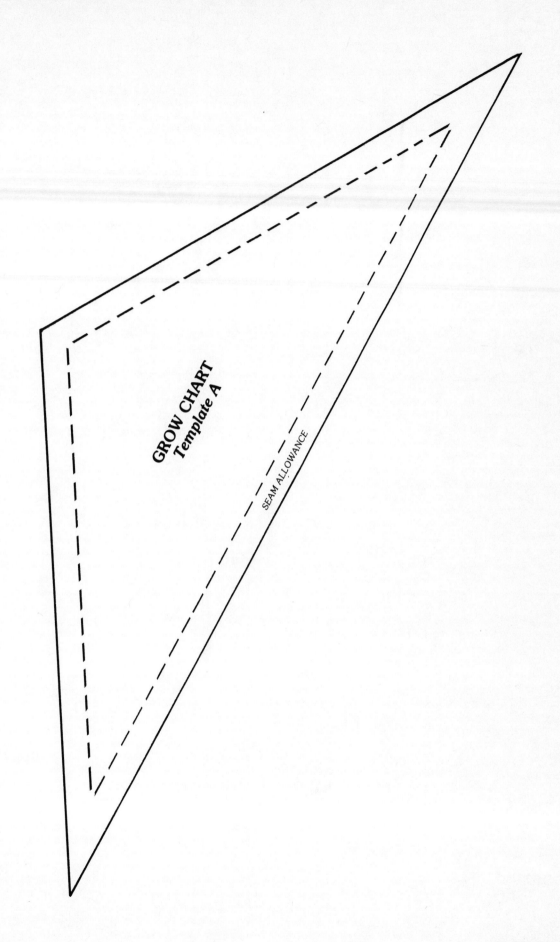

GROW CHART
Template A

SEAM ALLOWANCE

PLATE 9

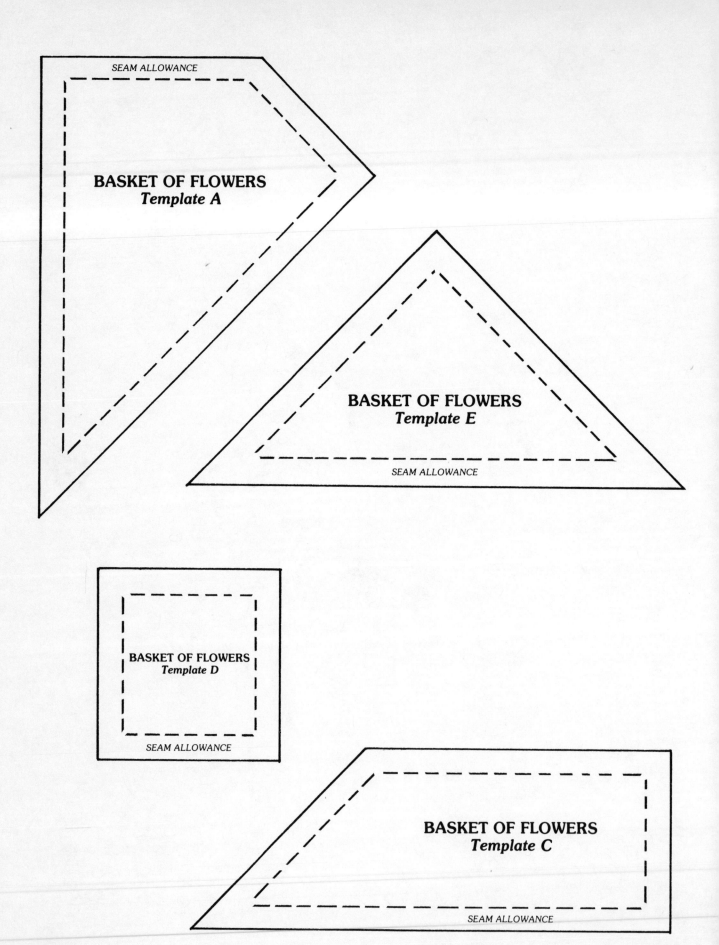

SEAM ALLOWANCE

BASKET OF FLOWERS
Template A

BASKET OF FLOWERS
Template E

SEAM ALLOWANCE

BASKET OF FLOWERS
Template D

SEAM ALLOWANCE

BASKET OF FLOWERS
Template C

SEAM ALLOWANCE

PLATE 10

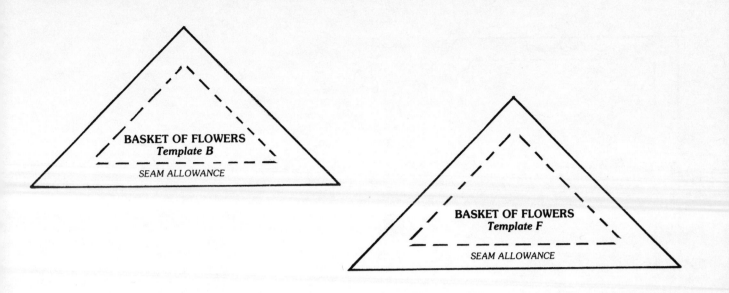

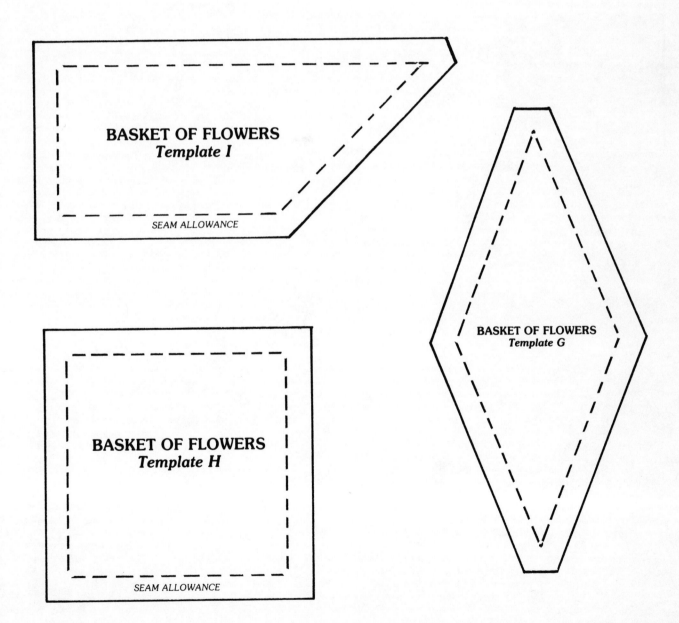

BASKET OF FLOWERS
Template B
SEAM ALLOWANCE

BASKET OF FLOWERS
Template F
SEAM ALLOWANCE

BASKET OF FLOWERS
Template I
SEAM ALLOWANCE

BASKET OF FLOWERS
Template G

BASKET OF FLOWERS
Template H
SEAM ALLOWANCE

PLATE 11

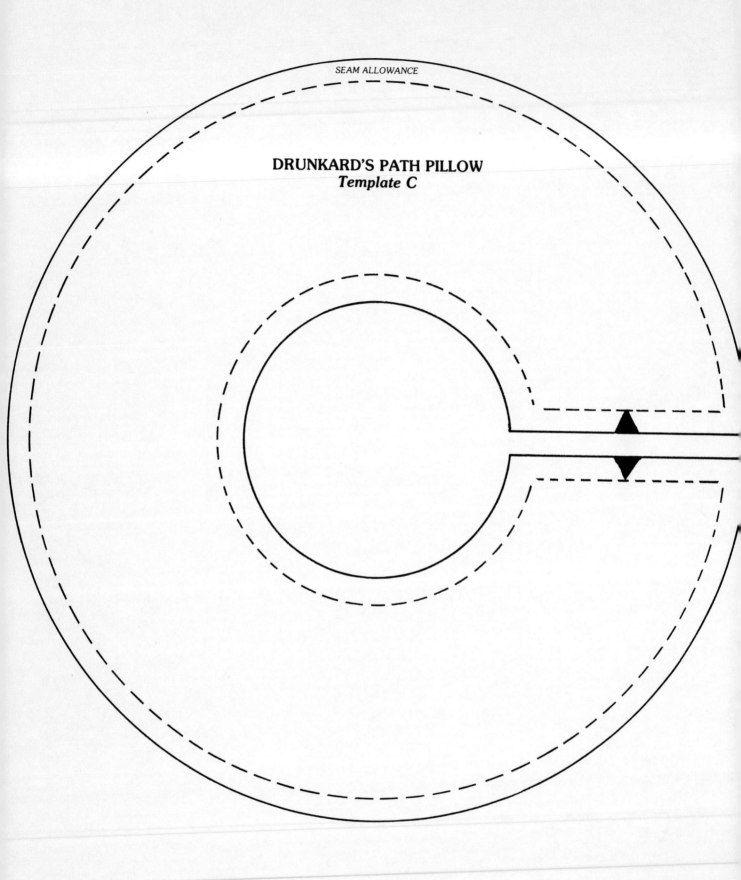

SEAM ALLOWANCE

DRUNKARD'S PATH PILLOW
Template C

PLATE 12

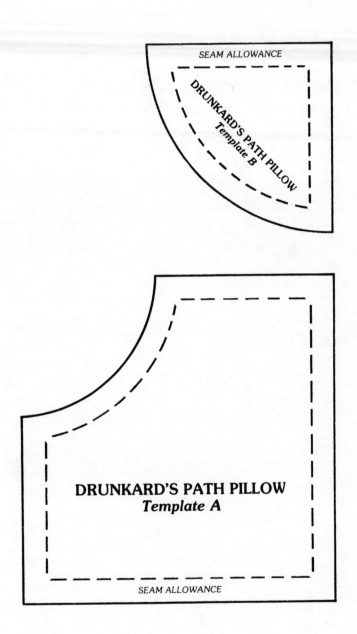

SEAM ALLOWANCE

DRUNKARD'S PATH PILLOW
Template B

DRUNKARD'S PATH PILLOW
Template A

SEAM ALLOWANCE

PLATE 13

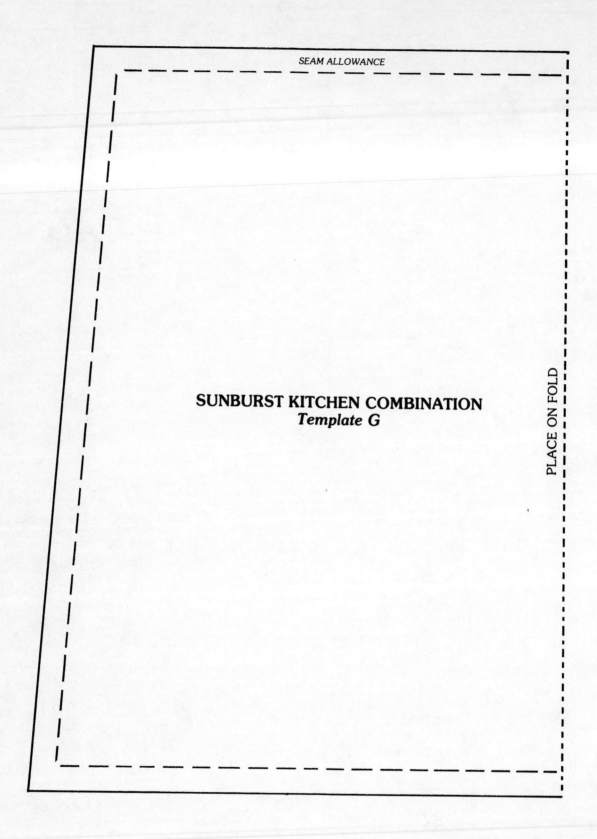

SEAM ALLOWANCE

SUNBURST KITCHEN COMBINATION
Template G

PLACE ON FOLD

PLATE 14

SUNBURST KITCHEN COMBINATION
Template F

SEAM ALLOWANCE

SUNBURST KITCHEN COMBINATION
Template D

SEAM ALLOWANCE

SUNBURST KITCHEN COMBINATION
Template C

SEAM ALLOWANCE

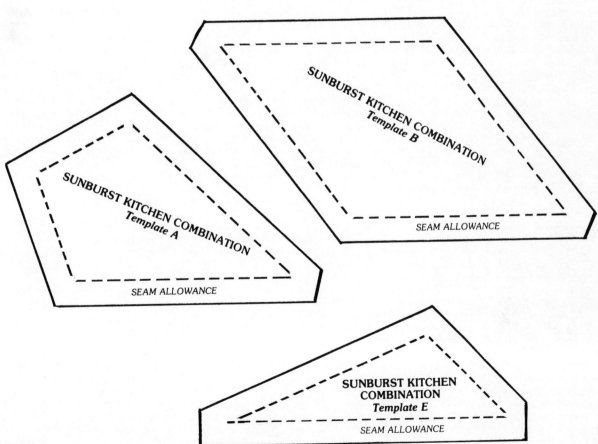

SUNBURST KITCHEN COMBINATION
Template B

SEAM ALLOWANCE

SUNBURST KITCHEN COMBINATION
Template A

SEAM ALLOWANCE

SUNBURST KITCHEN COMBINATION
Template E

SEAM ALLOWANCE

PLATE 15

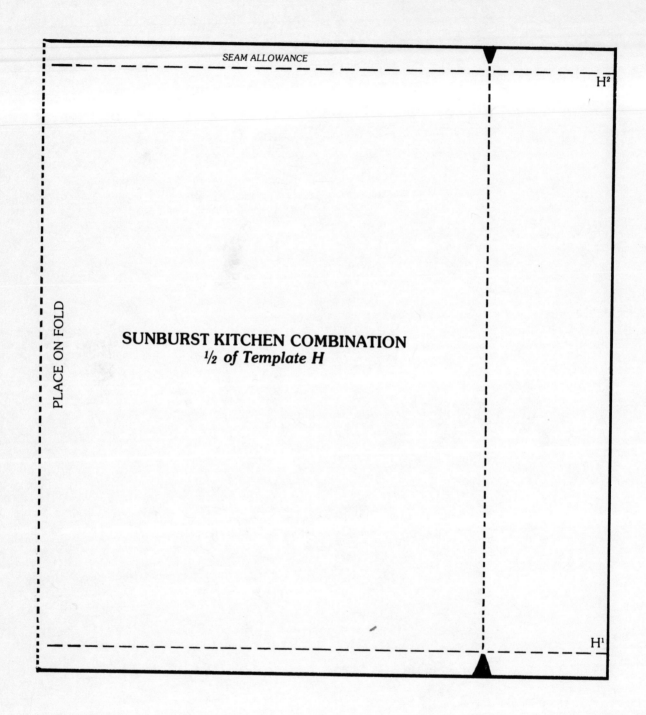

SEAM ALLOWANCE

H²

PLACE ON FOLD

SUNBURST KITCHEN COMBINATION
½ of Template H

H¹

PLATE 16

H²

SUNBURST KITCHEN COMBINATION
½ of Template H

H¹

PLATE 17

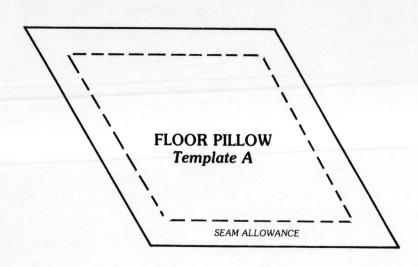

FLOOR PILLOW
Template A

SEAM ALLOWANCE

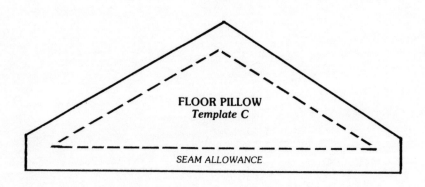

FLOOR PILLOW
Template C

SEAM ALLOWANCE

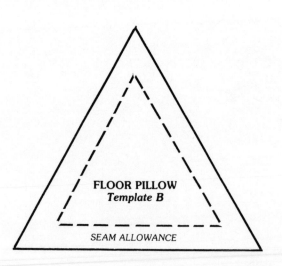

FLOOR PILLOW
Template B

SEAM ALLOWANCE

PLATE 18

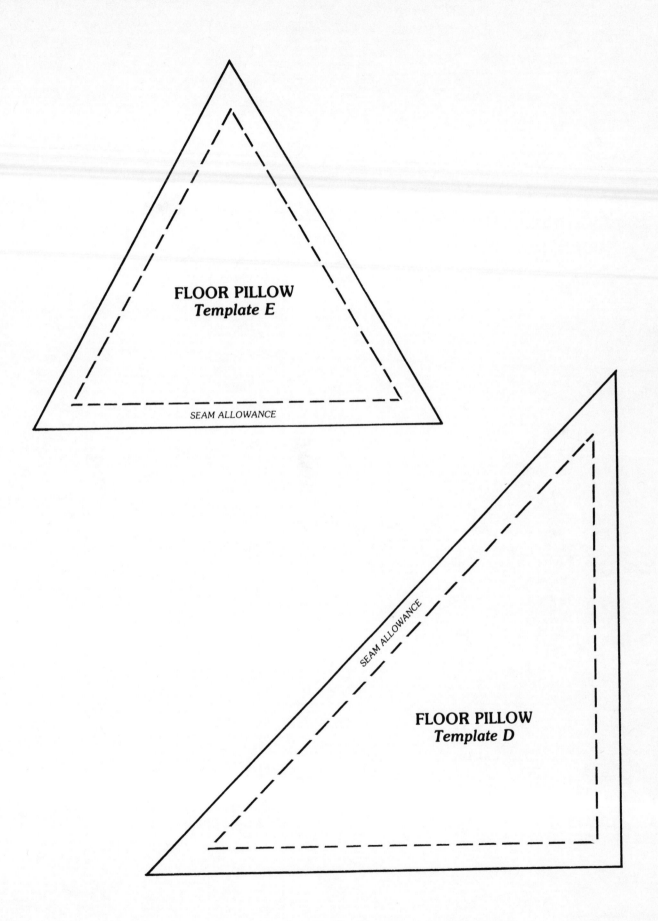

FLOOR PILLOW
Template E

SEAM ALLOWANCE

SEAM ALLOWANCE

FLOOR PILLOW
Template D

PLATE 19

SEAM ALLOWANCE

SOFA THROW
Template A

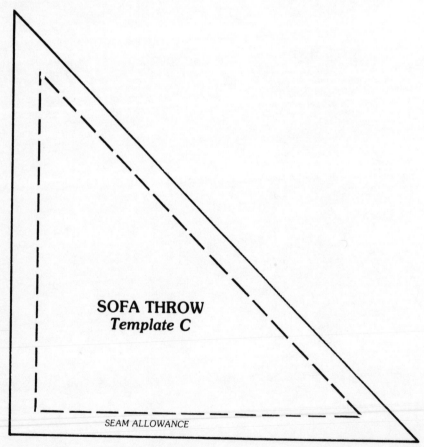

SOFA THROW
Template C

SEAM ALLOWANCE

PLATE 20

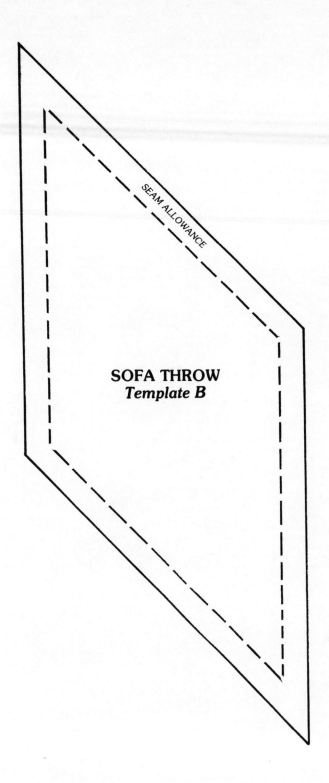

SEAM ALLOWANCE

SOFA THROW
Template B

PLATE 21

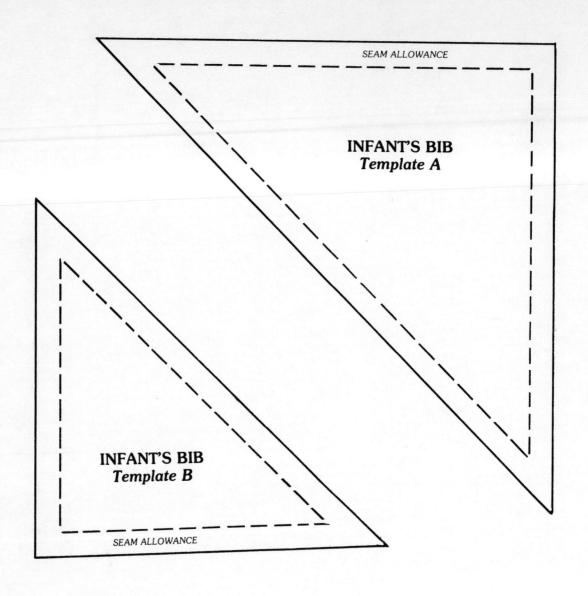

SEAM ALLOWANCE

INFANT'S BIB
Template A

INFANT'S BIB
Template B

SEAM ALLOWANCE

INFANT'S BIB
Template C

SEAM ALLOWANCE

PLATE 22

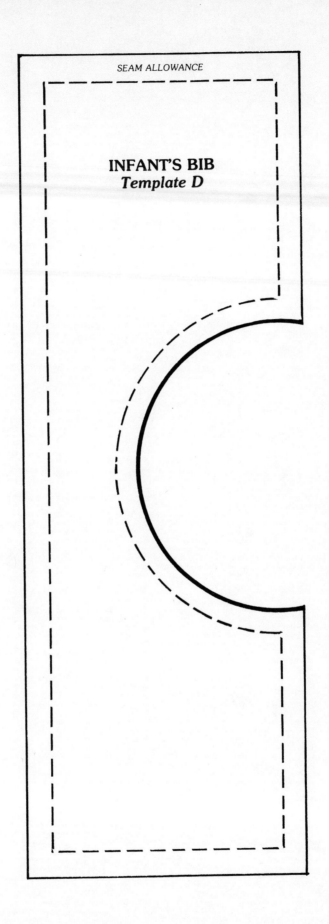

SEAM ALLOWANCE

INFANT'S BIB
Template D

PLATE 23

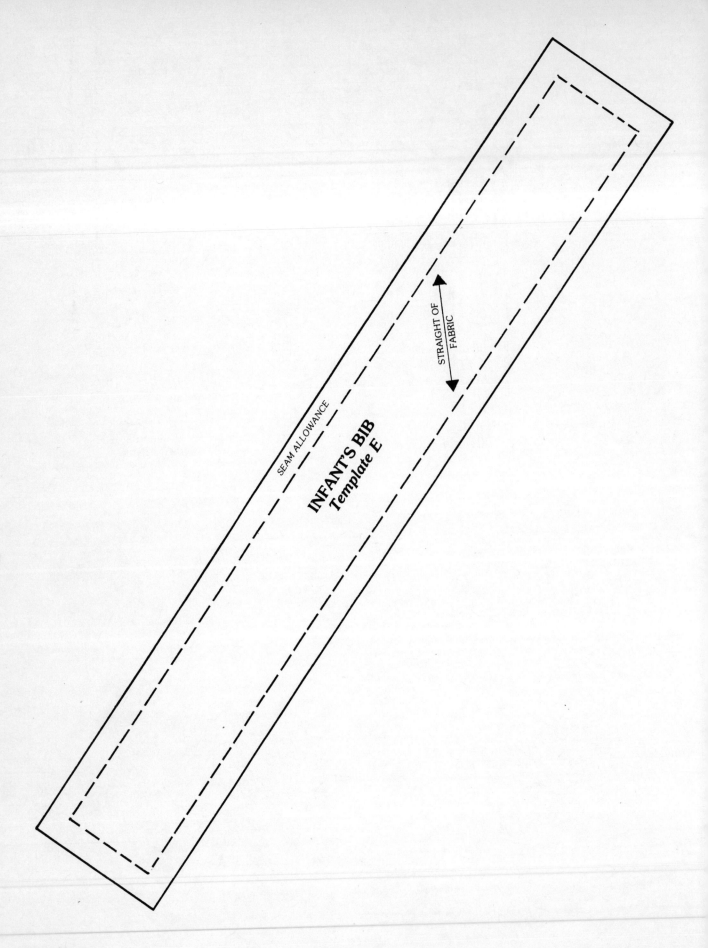

SEAM ALLOWANCE

INFANT'S BIB
Template E

STRAIGHT OF FABRIC

PLATE 24